Why did HIROSHIMA happen?

R. G. GRANT

Gareth Stevens
Publishing

Please visit our Web site, www.garethstevens.com. For a free color catalog of all our high-quality books, call toll free 1-800-542-2595 or fax 1-877-542-2596.

Library of Congress Cataloging-in-Publication Data

Grant, R. G.
  Why did Hiroshima happen? / R.G. Grant.
    p. cm. -- (Moments in history)
  Includes index.
  ISBN 978-1-4339-4163-4 (library binding)
  ISBN 978-1-4339-4164-1 (pbk.)
  ISBN 978-1-4339-4165-8 (6-pack)
  1. Hiroshima-shi (Japan)--History--Bombardment, 1945--Juvenile literature. 2. Capitulations, Military--Japan--History--20th century--Juvenile literature. 3. World War, 1939-1945--Japan--Juvenile literature. 4. World War, 1939-1945--United States--Juvenile literature. 5. Atomic bomb--History--Juvenile literature. I. Title.
  D767.25.H6G74 2011
  940.54'2521954--dc22
                    2010012464

First Edition

Published in 2011 by
Gareth Stevens Publishing
111 East 14th Street, Suite 349
New York, NY 10003

Series concept: Alex Woolf
Editor: Philip de Ste. Croix
Designer: Andrew Easton
Picture researcher: Thomas Mitchell
Project manager: Joe Harris

Photo credits: All the photographs in this book were supplied by Getty Images and are reproduced here with their permission, except cover image: Bettmann/CORBIS. The photographs appearing on the pages listed below are Time Life images. Time Life Pictures/Getty Images: 28, 30.

Printed in the United States of America

CPSIA compliance information: Batch #AS10GS: For further information contact Gareth Stevens, New York, New York at 1-800-542-2595.

SL001513US

CONTENTS

CHAPTER 1

THE BOMB IS DROPPED

Waking up on August 6, 1945, no one in Hiroshima could have dreamt what the day would bring. Hiroshima is a city on the island of Honshu in the south of Japan. That morning, Dr. Michihiko Hachiya wrote in his diary, "The hour was early, the morning still, warm, and beautiful."

Japan had then been at war with the United States and its allies for three and a half years, but the war was going badly for Japan and most Japanese cities had been badly damaged by American bombing raids. But Hiroshima, a port and industrial center with a population of around 300,000, had been largely untouched by the bombing. Japan's 2nd Army was based in the city and more than 40,000 soldiers were stationed there. But most of the population were women, children,

and old people, because the younger men were away fighting. On that fine summer morning, Hiroshima bustled with crowded streetcars trundling through busy streets, while soldiers performed their daily exercises outside their barracks. There had been an air-raid warning at 7:15, but nothing had happened and the all-clear followed. An hour later, few people paid much attention as three American bombers appeared flying high in the blue sky over the city. The bombers were B-29s from Group 509 of the U.S. Air Force. They had taken off from their base

For a period after Japan first entered the war in 1941-42, it conquered large parts of Asia and the Pacific. However, in the summer of 1944, the United States captured the Mariana Islands, including Tinian. This brought Japan within range of American B-29 bombers—making possible the atomic raids on Hiroshima and Nagasaki in 1945.

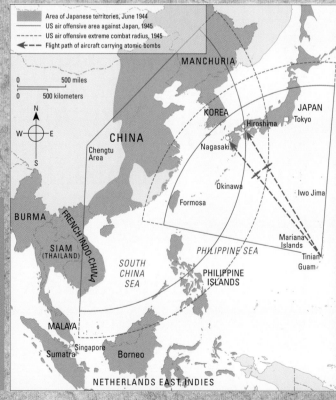

Area of Japanese territories, June 1944
US air offensive area against Japan, 1945
US air offensive extreme combat radius, 1945
Flight path of aircraft carrying atomic bombs

0   500 miles
0   500 kilometers

N W E S

MANCHURIA

KOREA

JAPAN

Hiroshima   Tokyo

CHINA

Chengtu Area

Nagasaki

Okinawa

Iwo Jima

Formosa

BURMA

FRENCH INDO-CHINA

SIAM (THAILAND)

SOUTH CHINA SEA

PHILIPPINE SEA

Mariana Islands

Tinian Guam

PHILIPPINE ISLANDS

MALAYA

Singapore   Borneo

Sumatra

NETHERLANDS EAST INDIES

The commander of the aircraft that dropped the atom bomb on Hiroshima, Colonel Paul W. Tibbets, waves to news photographers from the cockpit of his B-29 bomber before taking off on his fateful mission.

on Tinian Island in the Marianas at 2:45 A.M. local time at the start of a 1,500-mile (2,400-km) flight across the Pacific Ocean. Their mission was to drop the first atom bomb—a device many, many times more destructive than any weapon previously used in the history of warfare.

TOP SECRET

The man charged with leading the bombing mission was Colonel Paul W. Tibbets, the commander of Group 509. He had named his bomber *Enola Gay*, his mother's maiden name. The

The only bomber in the US Air Force then capable of flying the distance from Tinian Island to Japan and back was the Boeing B-29 Superfortress. Despite its four powerful engines, it had difficulty taking off with the 4.85-ton atom bomb on board, plus a full fuel load for the long journey.

development of the bomb had taken place in total secrecy. When they took off, even most of the *Enola Gay's* 12-man crew still did not know all the facts about the weapon they were carrying. But they did know that they were embarking on a vital mission to drop a bomb of massive explosive power. It had even been suggested that, if successful, the bomb would force Japan to surrender.

By this stage of the war, Japan's air defenses had been virtually destroyed, so the bomber's flight to Hiroshima was uneventful. The main risk to the success of the mission was the weather. The attack had to be carried out from high altitude, because otherwise the huge explosion would destroy the aircraft. But the ground had to be visible for the bomb to be targeted accurately. If it was cloudy, the mission would be aborted. Three other B-29s had set off in advance of *Enola Gay* to report back on weather conditions over Japan. The early air-raid warning in Hiroshima that day was triggered by one of these aircraft. They radioed Tibbets the news that bombing conditions at Hiroshima were perfect.

Aioi Bridge in the center of Hiroshima was the specific mission target. *Enola Gay* approached flying at 199 miles per hour (320 km/h) at an altitude of 5.9 miles (9.5 km). At one minute from the target, Tibbets ordered the crew to put on dark antiglare goggles to protect their eyes. At 8:15 local time, the bomb was released. Tibbets banked the B-29 sharply away from the target, trying to get as much distance as possible between the aircraft and the bomb before it exploded. A minute after it was dropped, the atom bomb airburst over the city.

When the crew looked back at Hiroshima, after the first shock waves had passed, they saw the city, in Tibbets's words, "hidden by that awful

View from the air

Sergeant Robert Caron, the tail gunner on the *Enola Gay*, recalled what he saw after the bomb exploded:

"The mushroom [cloud] itself was a spectacular sight, a bubbling mass of purple-gray smoke and you could see it had a red core in it and everything was burning inside… I saw fires springing up in different places, like flames shooting up on a bed of coals… It looked like lava or molasses covering the whole city, and it seemed to flow outward up into the foothills … so pretty soon it was hard to see anything because of the smoke."

Quoted in Richard Rhodes, *The Making of the Atomic Bomb* (Penguin, 1986)

cloud . . . boiling up, mushrooming and incredibly tall." The airmen had been eager to carry out an important task, and part of their immediate reaction was satisfaction that the mission had been accomplished successfully. Radar officer Lieutenant Jacob Beser's first thought was, "What a relief it worked." The B-29s flew back to Tinian, where the crew were welcomed home as heroes.

HIROSHIMA IN RUINS

On the ground, the moment of detonation was marked by an intense flash of light and a searing wave of heat. In that instant, thousands of people close to the explosion died, burned to a cinder or totally vaporized. All that was left of some of them was a shadow on a wall. Further from the center of the explosion, tens of thousands were blinded by the flash or suffered terrible burns. Then came a

Mission accomplished. Flight and ground crew are pictured at Tinian Airfield after the successful dropping of the bomb on Hiroshima by the *Enola Gay*.

blast wave that destroyed almost every building in an area of 7.5 square miles (19 sq. km). The force of the blast drove splinters of shattered glass and wood into people's bodies and many people were buried in the wreckage of ruined buildings. The sun was obscured and the sky became black with dust and debris. Violent winds roared through the city, setting up firestorms that flared unpredictably, trapping many victims attempting to find refuge from the catastrophe. Soon, a sinister black rain began to fall.

Survivors recalled the awful injuries that people endured. People wandered the streets with burned skin hanging from their bodies. Dr. Michihiko Hachiya's diary records victims whose "eyes, noses and mouths had been burned away" so that you could not tell the front of their heads from the back.

After the bombing of Hiroshima, local doctor Michihiko Hachiya wrote, "Nothing remained except a few buildings of reinforced concrete." About 70,000 of the 76,000 buildings in the city were damaged or destroyed.

A SECOND BOMB

Three days later, a second atom bomb was dropped on the city of Nagasaki. Five days later, Japan surrendered. From the Allies' point of view, these bombs helped to end the war with Japan. British wartime leader Winston Churchill described it as "a miracle of deliverance." Thousands of soldiers

VOICES FROM HISTORY

"A shattering flash filled the sky…"

One survivor of the Hiroshima bombing was Futaba Kitayama. She later recalled the moment the bomb exploded:

"…a shattering flash filled the sky. I was thrown to the ground as the whole world collapsed around me … I couldn't see anything. It was completely dark… All the skin came off my face, and then all the skin on my arms and hands fell off. The sky was black as night, and I ran homewards towards the Tsurumi River bridge. People by the hundreds were flailing in the river…"

Stephen Harper, *Miracle of Deliverance* (Sidgwick & Jackson, 1985)

WHY DID IT HAPPEN ?

Different perspectives

Arguments about the morality of using such a destructive weapon on civilian targets have raged ever since. In 1945, Paul Fussell was a young soldier preparing to fight in an invasion of Japan. When he and his fellow soldiers heard the news of the Hiroshima bombing, Fussell wrote, "we cried with relief and joy. We were going to live." In an article entitled "Thank God for the Atom Bomb," published in 1981, he argued that the bombing of Hiroshima was necessary to save American soldiers' lives.

Professor Michael Walzer replied to Fussell's article by denouncing the use of the atom bomb as totally immoral. He wrote, "The bombing of Hiroshima was an act of terrorism. . . . The goal was to kill enough civilians to shake the Japanese government and force it to surrender. And this is the goal of every terrorist campaign."

Enola Gay pilot Colonel Paul W. Tibbets never doubted that he had made the right decision. Almost half a century after the event, he wrote, "I had no problem with it. I know we did the right thing. . . ."

Paul Fussell and Michael Walzer, *The New Republic* magazine (1981); Paul Tibbets quoted in an interview with Studs Terkel, *The Guardian* (2002)

After the bomb had been dropped on Hiroshima, makeshift hospitals were set up in damaged buildings. Survivors suffering from cuts and burns took shelter in them. However, the surviving medical personnel did not know how to treat the radiation sickness which began to kill their patients.

waiting to fight or prisoners of war starving in Japanese camps believed that the atom bomb had ended the war and saved their lives.

However, the cost in human lives on the ground was awful. Precise figures for the number of people who died as a result of the Hiroshima bombing are not available. Initially it was estimated that about 80,000 people died either as a result of the heat flash and blast, or from exposure to gamma radiation released by the explosion, which killed victims in twenty to thirty days. The Hiroshima city government, however, claims that the true death toll was 140,000 by the end of 1945. Thousands more died from the longterm effects of radiation.

CHAPTER 2

UNCONDITIONAL SURRENDER

World War II was one of the bloodiest conflicts in history. By the time the bomb was dropped on Hiroshima in 1945, around 50 million people (most of them civilians) had already died in the war. The world had grown accustomed to killing on a scale unwitnessed in earlier times. The decision to use the bomb must be seen in this context.

The world went to war because of the actions of aggressive militarist governments that rose to power in Germany and Japan in the 1930s. In September 1939, Germany, ruled by Nazi dictator Adolf Hitler, invaded Poland. Britain and France, the leading democratic powers in Europe, responded by declaring war on Germany. The Germans defeated France in June 1940 and invaded the Soviet Union in June 1941.

In the Far East, the Japanese had ambitions to create an empire in Asia. Officially ruled by Emperor Hirohito, in the 1930s Japan was dominated by army and navy officers. In 1937, Japan attacked China, and in 1940, Japanese troops moved into parts of Southeast Asia. American president Franklin D. Roosevelt thought that America's economic power might be enough to put a stop to Japanese expansion. In the summer of 1941, the United States organized a blockade of the supply of oil to Japan. The Japanese army relied on imported oil to continue its operations. Japan's leaders had to decide whether to give up their ambitions of building an Asian empire or go to war with the United States. They chose war.

AMERICA IS ATTACKED

The naval station at Pearl Harbor in Hawaii was the base for the U.S. Pacific Fleet. On December 7, 1941, Japanese aircraft launched a preemptive strike from the air against the base. Three

This picture shows the ruins of Dresden, a city struck by Allied air raids in February 1945 as part of a devastating bombing campaign against targets in Germany. Tens of thousands of civilians were killed in Dresden alone.

The Japanese attack on Pearl Harbor on December 7, 1941, caught the American forces by surprise. American aircraft, unable to take off in time, are seen here wrecked and burning.

Pearl Harbor

On December 7, 1941, Japanese naval aircraft attacked the American Pacific naval base at Pearl Harbor, Hawaii, achieving total surprise. No formal declaration of war had been made. They had taken off from Japanese warships, including six aircraft carriers, that had sailed undetected in the first week of December to within flying range of the base. America's leaders knew that a war with Japan was likely to begin any day, but personnel at Pearl Harbor were not alerted to the threat. Eighteen U.S. ships were sunk, including four battleships; crucially, however, America's aircraft carriers were not in port and all survived. Around 3,500 American servicemen were killed. This sneak attack shocked and angered the American people. Americans often cited Pearl Harbor as a justification for showing no mercy to the Japanese.

days later, Germany declared war on the United States. The Americans were thus drawn into conflict in two theaters of war. In Europe and North Africa, they fought against Germany and its associates. America's main allies in the European theater were Britain and the Soviet Union. In the Pacific and Southeast Asia, the United States and Britain took on the Japanese. The Soviet Union did not join in the fight against Japan until very late in the war. In 1943, the Allies declared a policy of "unconditional surrender." This meant that they would not enter into peace negotiations to end the war. Germany and Japan would have to accept defeat and allow the Allies to occupy their countries.

The British and Americans regarded Germany's and Japan's rulers as evil and barbaric. They were prepared to resort to almost any means to win the war, including bombing enemy cities. Before they entered the war, America's leaders had been outspokenly critical of what Roosevelt called "the ruthless bombing from the air of civilians." But after the United States declared war, American

bombers joined with the Royal Air Force in devastating raids on German cities. The United States always claimed to be attacking military targets—including factories producing war equipment—but inevitably many thousands of civilians were killed in the raids. Broadly

11

speaking, public opinion in Britain and America supported the bombing of German cities, especially as the Germans themselves had bombed London and other European cities.

In the eyes of the Americans in World War II, the Japanese were the most hated of their enemies, more even than the Germans, and so they felt even less inhibition about bombing cities in Japan. From February 1942, around 110,000 people of Japanese origin, many of them full American citizens, were forcibly rounded up from the West Coast of the United States and detained in camps. Americans of German origin were not subjected to such treatment. Of course, Germany had not directly attacked the United States, but there was almost certainly an element of racism in the American attitude toward the Japanese. In an opinion poll conducted in the United States in December 1944, one in three people said they thought Japan should cease to exist as a country when the war

Members of a Japanese-American family in California await transfer to an internment camp in the United States in 1942. Most white Americans felt that the Japanese-Americans could not be trusted.

VOICES FROM HISTORY

Not human beings

American journalist John Hersey described the attitude of U.S. Marines towards the Japanese in an article describing the fighting on the Pacific island of Guadalcanal in 1942:

"Quite frequently you hear Marines say: 'I wish we were fighting against the Germans. They are human beings like us… But the Japs are like animals… They take to the jungle as if they had been bred there, and like some beasts you never see them until they are dead.'"

Quoted in Richard Rhodes, *The Making of the Atomic Bomb* (Penguin, 1986)

ended, and one in eight said that the entire Japanese population should be exterminated.

INHUMANE TREATMENT

The early stages of the Pacific war were marked by rapid Japanese advances and military success. The Japanese army swiftly conquered Singapore and the Philippines and pushed on as far as Indonesia and Burma. Many Allied soldiers were taken prisoner and reports soon surfaced of their mistreatment. Captured Allied soldiers were often starved, beaten, tortured, or executed.

About one in four Allied prisoners of the Japanese died in captivity. The Japanese were equally brutal toward fellow Asians, massacring large numbers of Chinese and Filipinos. After Pearl Harbor, regarded by the American public as a totally unprovoked attack, hatred of the Japanese was fanned by

By mid-1942, the Japanese armed forces had control of a vast area stretching from the islands of the central Pacific to Burma and from Manchuria to the Netherlands East Indies (Indonesia). The Japanese claimed to be liberating Asian people from rule by white people, but treated them brutally.

Territory controlled by the Japanese, 1942

accounts of such atrocities.

The fighting in the Pacific war was hard and merciless. The Japanese were prepared to die willingly for their emperor and their homeland and would often fight to the death rather than surrender. For their part, American soldiers were ruthless in return. They rarely took prisoners, mostly killing every "Jap" they could find. From 1943 on, the Americans drove the Japanese back across the Pacific island by island. Casualties on both sides mounted steeply as the fighting neared the mainland. From October 1944, Japanese airmen started to use "kamikaze" suicide tactics, deliberately crashing their aircraft onto the decks of Allied warships. In the face of such reckless courage, the Americans reasoned that Japan was unlikely to surrender until it was utterly crushed.

By November 1944, the advancing American forces had taken Pacific islands that lay within flight range of Japanese cities. The bombing raids from these bases did not have a major impact, however, until March 1945, when U.S. aircraft began to carry out mass raids at night using firebombs. These raids, ordered by Major General Curtis LeMay, were devastating. Japanese buildings caught fire easily, as they were mostly made of wood and paper. When 300 aircraft of the U.S. 20th Bomber Command attacked Tokyo on the night of March 9–10, they started a fire that destroyed 24 square miles (62 sq. km) of the city and may have killed as many as 100,000 people.

A MORAL DILEMMA

The ethics of bombing civilian targets aroused considerable public debate. In February 1945, Allied bombers—mostly British—had devastated the German city of Dresden, killing an estimated 60,000 people for no clear military purpose. Public protests followed. For this reason the United States insisted that its bombers were targeting military targets, such as barracks, ports, and

The cost in human lives

American plans for an invasion of the Japanese mainland were taking shape in the summer of 1945. Judging by the ferocity of the previous fighting, thousands of American soldiers would have died. After the war, the question of potential casualties was one of the main arguments used to justify the bombing of Hiroshima and Nagasaki. In 1947, former Secretary of War Henry Stimson claimed that the invasion would have cost a million American casualties. This, he argued, had been avoided by the use of the bombs. In the following years, others estimated that the bombing had prevented half a million American deaths.

However, historian Barton J. Bernstein does not agree. He discovered that in June 1945, U.S. military planners estimated that an invasion of Japan in November would cost 25,000 U.S. lives, while 21,000 more might die if a follow-up invasion were required in 1946. A further 170,000 Americans were expected to be wounded in the two invasions. Bernstein wrote: "The myth of 500,000 American lives saved thus seems to have no basis in fact." Nevertheless, a number of historians still point out that much higher casualty estimates were being mentioned by some senior generals at the time.

Barton J. Bernstein quoted in Michael J. Hogan (ed.) *Hiroshima in History and Memory* (Cambridge University Press, 1996)

A Japanese fighter plane comes in low as it prepares to crash into the hull of the American battleship, the USS *Missouri*. Suicide attacks like this were evidence of a fanatical patriotism.

factories, when they struck at Japanese cities.

During the spring and summer of 1945, the bombs rained down on Japan's cities. At the same time, the island of Okinawa witnessed the fiercest battle of the Pacific war. From April through June, some 12,500 American soldiers were killed and 36,500 wounded. Japanese killed in the battle for Okinawa numbered around 220,000, made up of almost equal numbers of soldiers and civilians. But Japan's will to fight was undiminished, and the predictions in the summer of 1945 were that the war would continue into 1946. However, in secret, a weapon of awesome power was being prepared: the atom bomb.

15

BIRTH OF THE BOMB

In the early years of the twentieth century, the work of a German-born Jew, the scientist Albert Einstein, revolutionized our understanding of physics. It was his theoretical work that ultimately led to the invention of the atom bomb. Einstein published his special theory of relativity in 1905. In it he argued that even a small amount of matter could theoretically be transformed into a huge amount of energy. All matter is composed of atoms, and by the 1930s physicists had begun to discover ways of unlocking some of the energy of atoms by a process of "fission," or splitting, that released energy from the atom's nucleus. In early experiments, uranium atoms were split. It was realized that, in principle, it would be possible to set up a chain reaction in which large numbers of atoms were split in a very short time. The amount of energy released would be vast—in other words, there would be a massive explosion.

By the time World War II broke out in Europe in 1939, the theory behind what became known as an "atom bomb" was well established. All the major countries involved in the war had scientists who knew that the creation of such a weapon was theoretically possible. But no one knew for certain if theory could be turned into practice; nor did they know how long such a project might take.

Nazi dictator Adolf Hitler was notorious for his hatred of Jews. After Hitler came to power in 1933, discrimination and harassment by the Nazi regime forced many leading

Albert Einstein was forced out of Germany by the Nazi government because he was Jewish. Here he and his daughter, Margaret, take the oath to become citizens of the United States in October 1940.

Einstein was so concerned by the danger posed by the atom bomb that he wrote this letter to President Roosevelt in August 1939, shortly before the outbreak of war in Europe, alerting him to its destructive power.

Jewish scientists working in Germany to flee abroad, mostly to Britain or the United States. Einstein himself had left Germany in 1932, choosing in 1933 to live and work in America.

THE FEAR OF A GERMAN BOMB

The thought that such a destructive weapon might be developed first by Germany was a constant fear for the scientific community around the world. When war broke out, Jewish and non-Jewish scientists were concerned that Hitler would use it to achieve world domination. As German physicist Rudolph Peierls said, "The thought of Hitler being in possession of such a weapon with nobody else being able to hit back was of course very frightening." The race to be first to build the bomb was on—and many felt that it was vital that Britain or the United States should win it. Einstein wrote to Roosevelt explaining that "extremely powerful bombs of a new

Albert Einstein
Old Grove Rd.
Nassau Point
Peconic, Long Island

August 2nd, 1939

F.D. Roosevelt,
President of the United States,
White House
Washington, D.C.

Sir:

Some recent work by E.Fermi and L. Szilard, which has been communicated to me in manuscript, leads me to expect that the element uranium may be turned into a new and important source of energy in the immediate future. Certain aspects of the situation which has arisen seem to call for watchfulness and, if necessary, quick action on the part of the Administration. I believe therefore that it is my duty to bring to your attention the following facts and recommendations:

In the course of the last four months it has been made probable - through the work of Joliot in France as well as Fermi and Szilard in America - that it may become possible to set up a nuclear chain reaction in a large mass of uranium,by which vast amounts of power and large quantities of new radium-like elements would be generated. Now it appears almost certain that this could be achieved in the immediate future.

This new phenomenon would also lead to the construction of bombs, and it is conceivable - though much less certain - that extremely powerful bombs of a new type may thus be constructed. A single bomb of this type, carried by boat and exploded in a port, might very well destroy the whole port together with some of the surrounding territory. However, such bombs might very well prove to be too heavy for transportation by air.

type" could be built. After receiving the letter in October 1939, Roosevelt responded by setting up a "uranium committee" to promote atom bomb research.

Initially, British scientists made the most progress. By the time the United States entered the war in December 1941, the British had already discovered how to set off a controlled atomic explosion. Their work was top secret, but once the United States became an ally, they shared their knowledge with the Americans. The British realized that they did not have the enormous resources that would be needed to build an atom bomb; the United States did.

Why Did Hiroshima Happen?

President Roosevelt granted the project to build an American atom bomb an unlimited budget. The program was code-named the Manhattan Project and was launched in December 1941. The military officer in overall charge was Brigadier General Leslie R. Groves, while American physicist Robert Oppenheimer was made scientific director. Groves later described his mission as "to get this thing done and used as fast as possible."

Scientists from around the world were recruited to work on the team, and many transferred across from the British bomb project. They worked in several locations, including Chicago, where America's first nuclear reactor was built in 1942. The main research site was at Los Alamos, an isolated place in the wilds of New Mexico. Eventually some 6,000 people—mostly scientists, technicians, and their families—were living and working there, largely cut off from contact with the outside world.

There was more to the Manhattan Project, however, than just scientific research and experiment. It was also a major engineering and industrial program that ultimately employed around 200,000 people across the United States. Most of them were kept in the dark about what they were working on. Despite the scale of the project, it was also kept a secret from the public and even from most American political and military leaders. In the same spirit of secrecy, the huge sum spent on the project—$2 billion in total—was hidden from the U.S. Congress. Congress members did not know that the project existed.

Progress is Made

Hard work gradually saw solutions found to the many problems that were encountered during development. Groves informed President Roosevelt in the summer of 1944 that the first atom bombs would be ready for use the following year. A special bomber force was established so that the air force would be ready to drop the bombs as soon as they were built.

In Germany, the picture was very different. German industry had been badly damaged by the Allies' bombing campaign and resources were scarce. The Germans decided that their atom bomb project was not a realistic

A deadly competition

Otto Frisch, one of the Manhattan Project scientific team, offered this explanation of their motivations:

"Why start on a project which, if successful, would end with the production of a weapon of unparalleled violence, a weapon of mass destruction such as the world had never seen? The answer was very simple. We were at war and . . . very probably some German scientists had had the same idea and were working on it."

Quoted in Richard Rhodes, *The Making of the Atomic Bomb* (Penguin, 1986)

The culmination of two years of intensive work on bomb design and assembly by Manhattan Project scientists and technicians: an atomic device is raised up a tower in the New Mexico desert in preparation for the world's first atomic test.

proposition and stopped work on it. The threat of a Nazi bomb, which had been the reason why the Manhattan Project was set in motion, had ceased to exist. In fact, by the end of 1944, both Germany and Japan were facing certain defeat.

Despite the likelihood of eventual victory in the war, American efforts to produce an atom bomb project were not halted. The leaders of the Manhattan Project were determined to produce the

Germany conceded defeat in 1945, bringing the war in Europe to an end. Here German general Alfred Jodl signs the unconditional surrender document at Rheims, France, on May 7, 1945.

bomb in time for it to be used against the enemy. The feeling was that if the war ended before the bomb was built, their efforts would be wasted, and it would be hard to justify the huge amount of money that had been spent on the project without the approval of Congress. People who knew about the bomb considered that using it might possibly end the war quickly by forcing a shattered enemy to surrender.

When it became clear that Nazi Germany was not capable of building an atom bomb and was losing the war, some scientists involved in the Manhattan Project began to question what they were doing. They also wondered why the atom bomb was being kept a secret from the Soviet Union, America's wartime ally. A few of

them were recruited as Soviet spies to pass on information on the project to the Soviet Union. But the majority of scientists did not express any particular concerns about plans to use the bomb against Japan.

DECISIONS ARE MADE
The defeat of Germany in May 1945 meant that only Japan remained as a possible target for the atom bomb. A committee chaired by U.S. Secretary of War Henry L. Stimson, the Interim Committee, was set up to advise the president about its use. Among its members were a panel of scientific advisers including Oppenheimer. The committee considered two alternatives to dropping the bomb without warning on a Japanese city. One idea was to demonstrate the power of the bomb by dropping it in a deserted place. The other was to tell the Japanese when the bomb was going to be dropped

and on which city, so the population could be evacuated first. However, neither of these options was approved by the committee. Its unanimous recommendation was that the bomb should be used without warning against Japan.

The task of deciding on a suitable target fell to another committee. This one was called the Target Committee and was chaired by Leslie Groves. The requirement was to select a military target, but this could encompass almost every Japanese town or city since most of the population was involved in the war effort in some manner or other. In order that the full destructive effect of the bomb might be seen, committee members focused on cities that were larger than the area the bomb was expected to destroy. Also, they needed to select cities that had not already been reduced to rubble by U.S. bombing

Dissenting Voices

A number of Manhattan Project scientists based in Chicago had doubts about the use of the bomb. In May and June of 1945, they wrote to U.S. Secretary of War Henry Stimson to voice their concerns. This document is known as the Franck Report after one of the scientists involved, James Franck.

The Franck Report emphasized the level of destruction that would accompany any future global conflict fought with atomic weapons. It recommended that the foundation for a general international agreement to give up the use of atomic weapons in the future could be established if the Americans renounced the use of the atom bomb against Japan. If America did drop the bomb on a Japanese city, other countries might turn away from the United States with "a wave of horror and repulsion sweeping over the rest of the world."

American political and military leaders ignored the opinions of the Chicago scientists.

The chairman of the Interim Committee, Henry L. Stimson. He had been a critic of the bombing of civilians, but as the U.S. secretary of war he approved the use of the atom bomb. He believed that it would shorten the war and so save lives.

raids in order to demonstrate the bomb's power to the fullest.

One target seemed ideal. Hiroshima had a port and an army base, which identified it as a legitimate military target. It was large enough and mostly undamaged. And it was flat, which meant that the blast would spread to maximum effect. Other targets were harder to find. Eventually Nagasaki was chosen. It was a significant industrial center, but its surrounding hills would limit the bomb's effect.

No conventional bombing raids were flown against the chosen cities while the Manhattan Project team made their final preparations. Two types of bomb were built. One, using uranium, was nicknamed Little Boy. It was not tested before the event because its technology was considered utterly reliable. The other bomb was called Fat Man. Scientists at Los Alamos were less sure that Fat Man would work because it used plutonium (a rare radioactive element). For this reason, a test explosion of a plutonium device

VOICES FROM HISTORY

The first explosion

The first atomic test at Alamogordo stunned observers. Robert Oppenheimer, the scientific director of the Manhattan Project, described his reactions:

"We waited until the blast had passed, walked out of the shelter, and then it was extremely solemn. We knew the world would not be the same. A few people laughed, a few people cried. Most people were silent. I remembered the line from the Hindu scripture, the Bhagavad Gita: . . . 'Now I am become death, the destroyer of worlds.' I suppose we all thought that, one way or another."

Quoted in Len Giovanetti and Fred Freed, *The Decision to Drop the Bomb* (Methuen, 1967)

The bomb dropped on Hiroshima was known as Little Boy. This atom bomb shares its design. Key parts of the bomb were delivered to Tinian Island in the Pacific in July 1945 aboard the USS *Indianapolis*, a warship that was sunk only three days after making the delivery.

WHY DID IT HAPPEN ?

Delivering the deadly proof

Was it necessary to drop the bomb on a populated city to demonstrate its terrible power? Opinions differed. The Franck Report (see page 21) suggested dropping it on "a desert or barren island" to avoid untold civilian deaths. Admiral Lewis Strauss, a member of the Interim Committee, felt the bomb should be dropped on "a large forest . . . not far from Tokyo." But Robert Oppenheimer, on the Interim Committee's Scientific Panel, disagreed. He did not think that a demonstration "was likely to induce surrender." He doubted that the Japanese would have been influenced by "an enormous nuclear firecracker detonated at great height and doing little damage."

The U.S. government did not accept the idea that the bomb should not be used on a "live" target. Secretary of State James Byrnes also rejected the idea of warning the Japanese when and where the bomb would be used. He later wrote: "We feared that, if the Japanese were told that the bomb would be used on a given locality, they might bring our boys who were prisoners of war to that area."

Strauss quoted in Gar Alperovitz, *Atomic Diplomacy* (Pluto Press 1994 edition); Oppenheimer quoted in Richard Rhodes, *The Making of the Atomic Bomb* (Penguin, 1986); Byrnes quoted in Len Giovanetti and Fred Freed, *The Decision to Drop the Bomb* (Methuen, 1967)

This is the moment when the world's first atomic explosion took place at Alamogordo, New Mexico, on July 16, 1945. A wave of heat struck the faces of observers more than 6 miles (10 km) away from the blast.

was scheduled.

The test took place just before dawn on July 16, 1945, at Alamogordo in the New Mexico desert. A device equivalent to over 19,800 tons (18,000 metric tons) of TNT was detonated. It produced the brightest flash of light ever seen on Earth and temperatures three times hotter than the core of the sun. As they watched the mushroom cloud rise more than 7.5 miles (12 km), the scientists and technicians present had mixed feelings. They were pleased that the test was a success. But the sense of the awesome power that they had unleashed on the world was chilling.

CHAPTER 4

THE FATEFUL DECISION

As a result of the death of President Roosevelt on April 12, 1945, the political map in the United States had to be redrawn. Vice President Harry S. Truman, a relatively inexperienced political leader, stepped into the White House. The Manhattan Project had been kept such a top secret that Truman had not known anything about it until he assumed the presidency.

Germany had by now surrendered.

Berlin fell to advancing Allied troops in May 1945, and Nazi dictator Adolf Hitler committed suicide. In this scene, a convoy of Soviet army trucks drives through the ruins of the city. Relations between the Soviet Union and its wartime allies worsened soon after the defeat of Germany.

Therefore, the two big issues that Truman and his advisers faced were: how to defeat Japan as quickly as possible; and how America's future relationship with its wartime ally, the Soviet Union, would develop in peacetime. Soviet forces under the command of dictator Joseph Stalin had played a leading role in the Allied victory over Germany, but by the summer of 1945, relations between the Soviets and the Americans were turning sour. The country of Poland was a particular bone of contention, because the Soviet Union wanted to impose Communist rule there against the wishes of a large part of the Polish population.

Stalin is let into the secret

The Americans and British hoped that the revelation of their new secret weapon would come as a major shock and surprise to Stalin. At the Potsdam Conference, on July 24, Truman casually mentioned to the Soviet leader that the United States possessed a new weapon "of unusual destructive force." Stalin's unemotional response disappointed him. Stalin calmly welcomed the news and hoped that they would make "good use" of the weapon against the Japanese. In fact, spies at Los Alamos had passed on intelligence and Stalin already knew about the bomb, although he probably did not appreciate its full power and significance until the destruction of Hiroshima.

The leaders of the three major Allied powers at the opening of the Potsdam Conference in July 1945. Left to right: British prime minister Winston Churchill, American president Harry Truman, and Soviet dictator Joseph Stalin. During the conference, news came through that the Labour Party had defeated the Conservatives in a general election and Clement Attlee replaced Churchill as prime minister of Great Britain.

THE POTSDAM CONFERENCE

In the summer of 1945, the thoughts of the Allied leaders began to turn toward the shape of international relations in the postwar world. A conference was arranged at Potsdam, on the outskirts of Berlin, Germany, and in July Truman, Stalin, and Churchill met there. On the agenda was the future political direction of Europe and how best to bring the war with Japan to an end.

Truman and his secretary of state, James F. Byrnes, realized that their new secret weapon—the atom bomb—would give them a strong hand to play when dealing with Stalin. As if on cue, news came through of the successful test at Alamogordo at the very start of the Potsdam Conference.

The United States had argued that one of the outcomes of the Potsdam Conference should be Stalin's agreement to turn his military forces against Japan. The Soviet Union had not committed forces to the Pacific war while fighting Germany, but the Soviets

25

U.S. Marines fighting on the Japanese island of Okinawa in May 1945. U.S. forces suffered very heavy casualties in their drive toward Japan, and American leaders feared that an eventual invasion of the Japanese mainland would cost tens of thousands more soldiers' lives.

had promised to declare war on Japan once the Germans were defeated. Now the Americans wanted them to be true to their word.

However, in private, Truman and Byrnes were having second thoughts. With the atom bomb almost ready, perhaps the United States could make Japan surrender quickly and win the war in the Far East without Soviet assistance. After all, if the Soviets

helped to defeat the Japanese, they would certainly want to extend their power and influence in the Far East. Truman was not sure which would be the better outcome. On July 18, when Stalin agreed to go to war with Japan the following month, the president wrote to his wife, "I've gotten what I came for." Yet in conversations with Byrnes he revealed that he hoped that the bomb might make the Japanese surrender before the Soviets got involved in the fighting.

The mood in Japan was also conflicted. Despite outward shows of defiance and declarations of national unity, in private the Japanese government was split in its attitude to prolonging the war. Some leading figures such as Foreign Minister Shigenori Togo were convinced that Japan's position was hopeless and wanted to negotiate an immediate end to the fighting. But others, including Minister of War General Korechika Anami, were determined that Japan should fight to the finish. From June 1945 on, Emperor Hirohito tentatively sided with those in favor of negotiation.

NO PEACE WITHOUT SURRENDER
In fact, the disagreements inside the

Japanese government were being communicated to the Allied leaders. Japanese codes had been cracked by American spies and secret messages, such as directives to Japanese embassies in foreign cities, were being intercepted. As a result, the emperor's support for the idea of using the neutral Soviet Union as a go-between in peace negotiations with the Allies was known. But the Allies were also aware that even

Japanese politicians bow to Emperor Hirohito during a session of the Japanese parliament in 1945.

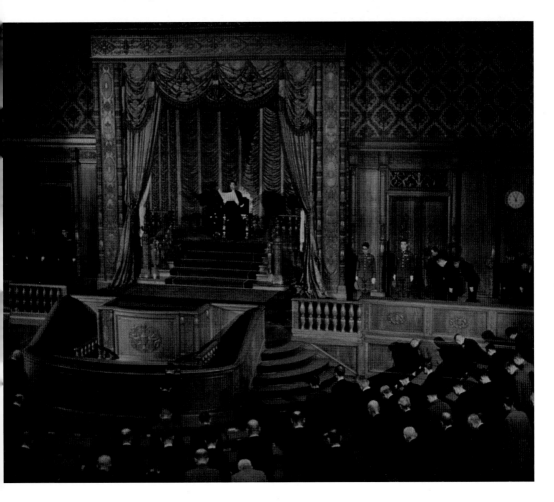

Japanese buildings were particularly vulnerable to fire because many of them were made of wood and paper. Attacking by night, hundreds of B-29 bombers dropped incendiary bombs that started huge firestorms. From March 1945, American bombing raids devastated Japanese cities.

those Japanese leaders in favor of peace negotiations still wanted to avoid actual surrender. In one intercepted message sent to the Japanese ambassador in Moscow in July, Togo said: "It is His Majesty's heart's desire to see the swift termination of the war. . . However, as long as England and America insist on unconditional surrender our country has no alternative but . . . an all-out effort for the sake of survival and the honor of the homeland." A negotiated peace with the Japanese was not an option that the Allies favored. For them, only total surrender would do.

Various military options for defeating Japan were on the table and they were reviewed by Allied military and political leaders in the summer of 1945. The heads of the U.S. Army, Navy, and Air Force each maintained that his own service could win the war. The Air Force argued that its bombing raids would devastate every Japanese city and force Japan to give in. Army commanders wanted to invade, arguing that only the occupation of at least part of the country by Allied troops would finally break the Japanese will to resist. The Navy proposed a stranglehold by blockading Japanese ports. The population would starve for lack of imported food and its industries would collapse without imported raw materials. Japan would be on its knees.

Truman's solution was to proceed with all of these strategies at the same time. The Navy would blockade Japan; the Air Force would bomb the cities; and the Army would mount an invasion of Kyushu, southern Japan, in November 1945. Plans were also drawn up for a follow-up invasion of central Japan in

Eisenhower's opposition

General Dwight D. Eisenhower was dismayed when told by Secretary of War Stimson about the decision to use the atom bomb against Japan. He later described his reaction:

"I was getting more and more depressed just thinking about it. Then he asked for my opinion, so I told him I was against it on two counts. First, the Japanese were ready to surrender and it wasn't necessary to hit them with that awful thing. Second, I hated to see our country be the first to use such a weapon."

Quoted in Richard Rhodes, *The Making of the Atomic Bomb* (Penguin, 1986)

March 1946, if it was needed. The U.S. military anticipated that the invasion of Kyushu would probably cost the lives of around 25,000 American servicemen. If a second invasion were needed, it was estimated that an additional 21,000 Americans would die.

Even at this pivotal moment, the existence of the atom bomb was kept a secret. Many senior American military commanders knew nothing about it until they were told at Potsdam in July. Those who had been let into the secret remained very skeptical about "secret weapons." They feared that either it would fail or that when it exploded it would prove to be much less powerful

General Dwight D. Eisenhower was one of the most powerful commanders in the U.S. military during World War II. In June 1945, he had been greeted as an American hero for leading the campaign that defeated Germany.

than was predicted.

Some military commanders expressed their reservations as a matter of principle. Both Admiral William D. Leahy, the U.S. Chief of Staff, and General Dwight D. Eisenhower, the Supreme Commander of Allied Forces in Europe, voiced their moral doubts in private. But no formal meeting of American military and political leaders was ever convened to discuss whether or not it was the correct decision to use the bomb.

LITLE BOY AND FAT MAN

Away from the political maneuverings at Potsdam, Groves pushed on with all possible speed with plans to drop the bomb. Paul Tibbets's B-29 bombers were already stationed on Tinian Island, and the materials for the first bomb were shipped there in the summer of 1945. Groves let Truman know that the first bomb (Little Boy) would be ready for use in early August. The second (Fat Man) would be ready shortly afterward, with a third bomb becoming available

VOICES FROM HISTORY

"Not women and children"

Truman's diary from the Potsdam Conference reveals his unease with the idea that the atom bomb was going to be used against civilians. Although he knew that the bomb was to be dropped on the city of Hiroshima, on July 25, Truman wrote:

"Military objectives and soldiers and sailors are the target and not women and children. Even if the Japs are savages, ruthless, merciless and fanatic, we as the leader of the world for the common welfare [are not]. The target will be a purely military one."

Quoted in Michael J. Hogan (ed.) *Hiroshima in History and Memory* (Cambridge University Press, 1996)

later in the month. On July 25, Truman formally authorized the use of atom bombs against Japan.

On July 26, the Allies issued the Potsdam Declaration, which called on the Japanese to proclaim the unconditional surrender of its armed forces and to accept occupation. This document sought to reassure the Japanese that the Allies did not intend to exterminate them or occupy their territories permanently, but it pulled no punches. An early draft stated that the Allies might allow Hirohito to stay on the throne, but this text was cut out of the final version. The declaration ended: "We call upon the government of Japan to proclaim now the

On Tinian Island, the Fat Man atomic bomb—later dropped on Nagasaki—was assembled and prepared for operational use.

Why was the bomb dropped?

President Truman's justification for dropping the atom bomb was made public on August 9, 1945, in an address to the American people: "We have used it in order to shorten the agony of war, in order to save the lives of thousands and thousands of young Americans."

Later historians expressed their doubts, however. In the 1960s, Gar Alperovitz argued that the main reason the bombs were dropped was not to end the war, but to alarm the Soviet Union. Martin J. Sherwin supported this view in *A World Destroyed*. Sherwin argued that Truman held out for unconditional surrender—which he knew the Japanese would reject—because "he preferred to use the atomic bomb" to reveal its power to the Soviets.

Today, most historians agree that U.S. leaders knew that relations with the Soviet Union would be affected by the impact of dropping the bomb. But most also believe that the straightforward hope of bringing about the defeat of Japan more rapidly by inflicting the heaviest possible blow lay behind the decision to drop the bomb.

Truman quoted in Michael J. Hogan (ed.) *Hiroshima in History and Memory* (Cambridge University Press, 1996); Martin J. Sherwin, *A World Destroyed* (Knopf, 1975)

Stalin (in white) and Truman (far left) attend a round-table meeting at the Potsdam Conference. Truman hoped that U.S. possession of the atom bomb would force the Soviet dictator to adopt a softer line on issues such as the future of Poland.

unconditional surrender of all Japanese armed forces. . . . The alternative for Japan is prompt and utter destruction."

Critics have attacked the Potsdam Declaration for two main reasons. Some maintain that if the Americans had allowed the Japanese emperor to remain on the throne, Japan might have surrendered. It has also been argued that the warning about the new weapon that was about to hit Japan was not explicit enough—the reference to "prompt and utter destruction" was simply too vague.

In any event, on July 28, Japanese prime minister Kantaro Suzuki rejected the Potsdam Declaration out of hand, calling it a "rehash" of earlier demands for unconditional surrender that should be ignored. The dropping of the atom bomb on Hiroshima was inevitable from then on.

CHAPTER 5

JAPAN SURRENDERS

In August 1945, the writing was on the wall for Japan—the war was lost. The U.S. Navy had sunk almost all of their ships—both merchant vessels and warships—and the U.S. Air Force was bombing their cities without meeting significant resistance. The surrender of Nazi Germany in May had left Japan without a single ally in the world. However, Japanese forces were still in control of Korea, much of China, and Southeast Asia. And the Japanese people were prepared to fight to the last in a final desperate defense of their homeland.

Emperor Hirohito's position was ambiguous. In public, he urged the entire nation to prepare for total resistance to the enemy that would "achieve the goals of the war." But privately he could see the benefit of entering peace negotiations. His military leaders had drawn up plans to resist an Allied invasion by directing troops to adopt suicide tactics, not only in the air but on sea and land. The government-controlled newspapers urged the Japanese people to be prepared to die for their emperor.

Japan's political and military leaders were surprised and confused when they heard about the dropping of the atom bomb on Hiroshima on August 6. The type of bomb used was unclear and accurate reports of the extent of the destruction were not available. Communications between the Japanese

Japanese children pick their way through the ruined streets of Hiroshima. Their face masks are a barrier against the smell of rotting corpses.

capital, Tokyo, and Hiroshima had been severed by the immense explosion. Finally, on the morning of August 8, Japan's leaders received confirmation that a single bomb was responsible for the destruction of an entire city.

A bad situation then worsened because the Soviet Union declared war on Japan. Over a million Soviet troops had been stationed along the border between the Soviet Union and Japanese-occupied Manchuria. At 1:00 A.M. on August 9, the Soviets attacked, pouring across the border.

THE TIPPING POINT

The combination of the Soviet invasion and the annihilation of Hiroshima

VOICES FROM HISTORY

A population without hope

Koichi Kido, the Japanese emperor's chief adviser, gave a graphic account of the state of his country in summer 1945:

"The cities of Japan were being burned by bombings. . . . At least one city and at times two were being turned into ashes daily. . . . The food situation was becoming worse and worse. Under such conditions even the soldiers had not much to eat. There was nothing in Japan. . . . With winter ahead . . . tens of millions of people [faced] dying a dog's death from hunger and exposure."

Quoted in Len Giovanetti and Fred Freed, *The Decision to Drop the Bomb* (Methuen, 1967)

The Japanese defenses on the border of Manchuria were unable to resist the Soviet onslaught on August 9, 1945.

proved decisive in persuading the Japanese political and military leadership that the war must be brought to an end as a matter of urgency. The Japanese Supreme War Council met in Tokyo at 11 A.M. on August 9 to consider acceptable terms of surrender. Foreign Minister Togo was adamant that Japan must insist on just one condition: that the emperor remain on his throne. The majority of the council, however, wanted to hold out for other concessions, including agreement that Japan would not be occupied by Allied troops.

While they were deliberating, a second atom bomb was dropped, this time on the city of Nagasaki. The use of a second bomb so soon after Hiroshima has aroused criticism, since the Japanese government were not given enough time to respond to the first attack. However, Groves had been directed to continue dropping atom

Sweeney commanded the B-29 carrying the second bomb, and his aircraft flew through storms on its way from Tinian to Japan. Sweeney's orders were to drop the bomb on the city of Kokura, but when he arrived over the target it was obscured by thick clouds. Sweeney circled above Kokura hoping for a break in the clouds, but eventually decided to divert to his secondary target, the port city of Nagasaki. This was also blanketed by clouds, but the B-29 was running out of fuel, so Sweeney decided to drop the bomb anyway, in the general direction of the target zone that lay hidden below.

FAT MAN

The second bomb used different explosive technology. It was a plutonium device like the one tested at Alamogordo. Bearing the code-name Fat Man, it exploded at 11:02 A.M., about 1.5 miles (2.5 km) from its target. The death toll in Nagasaki is estimated at between 35,000 to 80,000. The geography of the city explains why fewer people were killed here than at Hiroshima. Nagasaki was built on a series of hills and valleys, and the hills surrounding the valley above which Fat Man exploded sheltered other parts of the city from the full effect of the blast and radiation.

In Tokyo, the Japanese leadership remained unable to resolve the deadlock over surrender terms throughout August 9, even after they received reports about Nagasaki. Minister of War Korechika Anami and the army and navy chiefs of staff were adamant that the country could fight on. It needed the

The mushroom cloud of the Fat Man atomic bomb over Nagasaki on August 9, 1945. The bomb was dropped from a B-29 nicknamed Bock's Car, piloted by Major Charles W. Sweeney.

bombs on Japan until the Japanese surrendered or until the president halted the bombing missions. The attack on Nagasaki had been scheduled for August 11, but the date was moved up to August 9 because weather forecasts suggested that the weather over Japan might be too bad by the 11th.

Even by August 9, weather conditions had deteriorated. Major Charles W.

intervention of the emperor to break the deadlock. A meeting was convened in an underground bomb shelter at the imperial palace, and at 2 A.M. on the morning of August 10, Hirohito declared himself in favor of immediate surrender because, if not, "the Japanese race would perish." The Allies were told that surrender terms would be accepted as long as "the prerogatives of His Majesty as a Sovereign Ruler" were not affected. In other words, Hirohito must remain on the throne.

Negotiation of Terms

The position of Hirohito posed a problem for Truman. Public opinion in the United States was strongly opposed to the Japanese emperor. Many of the population considered him as evil as Hitler, and one opinion poll revealed that one in three Americans wanted the emperor hanged as a war criminal. So a cautious reply was formulated that skirted around the issue of Hirohito's future. It stated that, after surrender, the emperor would come under the authority of the Allied supreme

The hills that surrounded Nagasaki absorbed some of the bomb blast, but the scale of destruction in the immediate vicinity of the target zone was immense. In the valley that took the full force of detonation, only a few concrete buildings were left standing.

TURNING POINTS IN HISTORY

The "cruel bomb"

For the first time, on the night of August 14–15, 1945, Emperor Hirohito prepared to address his people personally via a radio broadcast. He recorded a message informing Japan of the decision to surrender. He openly acknowledged that "the war situation has developed not necessarily to Japan's advantage" and made specific reference to the "cruel" atom bombs that had caused "incalculable" damage which had made it necessary to "endure the unendurable." Some army officers attempted to seize the recording to prevent its transmission, but they failed. The speech was broadcast at noon on August 15. This was the first time that ordinary people had heard the sacred emperor's voice. They found his ornate way of speaking very hard to understand. As the message began to sink in, a sense of shock developed. Many people were in tears. In his diary, Hiroshima doctor Hachiya observed that for him the surrender "produced a greater shock than the bombing of our city."

commander and that in due course the Japanese people would be free to choose their own form of government. The Japanese leadership was divided in its response—some were prepared to accept the terms while others were not.

A third atom bomb was now ready for shipment to Tinian Island, but Truman balked at the idea of using it. The president confessed that "the thought of wiping out another 100,000 people was too horrible." However, some of the heaviest conventional bombing raids of the war flown as air attacks on Japan were maintained.

The surrender negotiations were conducted in strict secrecy. The Japanese people knew nothing about them and, in fact, most were still prepared to fight on. Even the population of Hiroshima stood firm. According to the diary of Hiroshima doctor Michihiko Hachiya, on August 11, a rumor that Japan had retaliated with atom bomb attacks on American cities spread around a hospital that was

The formal surrender of Japan took place on board the battleship USS *Missouri* on September 2, 1945, more than two weeks after Emperor Hirohito had announced the decision to surrender. The Japanese delegation shown here met with U.S. General Douglas MacArthur.

looking after bomb victims. Immediately "everyone became cheerful and bright" and some patients "began singing the victory song."

Emperor Hirohito knew better than this. On August 14, he directed Japanese political and military leaders to accept the Allied terms. The country must "bear the unbearable." Some army officers attempted to mount a military coup to prevent the shame of surrender, but senior officers remained loyal to the emperor, and the coup attempt failed. At noon on August 15, Hirohito broadcast his radio message telling the Japanese people that the war was over.

Many Japanese people were shocked by the decision to surrender. These Japanese prisoners of war stand with their heads bowed after hearing the emperor's broadcast on August 15, 1945.

WHY DID IT HAPPEN

Was surrender inevitable?

In August 1945, most people accepted that the immediate cause of Japan's surrender was the use of the atom bomb. They welcomed the fact that there was no longer a need to invade Japan in November. However, the United States Strategic Bombing Survey, published shortly after the end of the war, stated that "in all probability prior to November 1, 1945, Japan would have surrendered even if the atom bombs had not been dropped, even if Russia had not entered the war, and even if no invasion had been planned or contemplated."

Most historians writing since 1945 have agreed that Japan was already facing defeat at the time the bombs were dropped. But opinions differ about how close Japan was to surrender. Barton J. Bernstein, for example, wrote that it was "likely," but "far from definite," that the war could have ended that summer without the atomic bombings. And the resistance of the Japanese leadership also had to be overcome. Koichi Kido, Hirohito's chief adviser in summer 1945, believed that without the bomb it would have been difficult to get Japan's military leaders to accept the need for surrender. He said, "The presence of the atomic bomb made it easier for us politicians to negotiate peace. Even then the military would not listen to reason."

Bernstein quoted in Michael J. Hogan (ed.) *Hiroshima in History and Memory* (Cambridge University Press, 1996); Kido quoted in Len Giovanetti and Fred Freed, *The Decision to Drop the Bomb* (Methuen, 1967)

CHAPTER 6

A PERILOUS NEW AGE

One of the first and most obvious signs of Japan's defeat was the appearance of Allied occupying troops in the country at the end of August 1945. These people saw the effects of the atom bombs on Hiroshima and Nagasaki firsthand. One American sailor, Osborn Elliot, later described the scene in Hiroshima, with "women and children . . . sitting on the rubble that was once their homes" and many people wandering about "with scars on their faces."

Casualties of the atomic bombing mounted remorselessly through late August and September. Thousands were dying and most were victims of exposure to the nuclear radiation released by the bomb. The first symptom of this "radiation sickness" was hair loss. This was followed by diarrhea and fever. White blood cells, an essential part of the body's defenses

Barely two months into the occupation, American servicemen join Japanese people shopping for goods salvaged from bombed-out buildings in Tokyo in October 1945.

against infection, were also wiped out. The sheer scale of this unforeseen catastrophe overwhelmed the few doctors who had survived in Hiroshima and Nagasaki. They were virtually powerless to help the victims.

Both Hiroshima and Nagasaki rose again from the ashes of their destruction, eventually growing into thriving modern communities. This picture was taken in 1955, and it shows that Hiroshima had already been extensively rebuilt.

To assert their control over what was potentially still a hostile country, the Allied occupation forces censored the Japanese media strictly. For three years after the war, the censors blanked out any mention of the effects of the bombing on Hiroshima and Nagasaki. The survivors fared no better. They were left to rebuild their lives as best they could without any special help from the authorities to deal with the aftereffects of the bombing: sickness, bereavement, disfigurement, or psychological trauma.

A PERIOD OF RECOVERY

Slowly, in the years immediately after the war, Japan began to find its feet again. The occupation came to an end in April 1952 and a general election returned a democratic system of government. Emperor Hirohito remained as the constitutional monarch. And in a reversal of the old world order, the Japanese now became the Americans' allies—the new enemy was the Soviet Union. The 1950s and 1960s also saw Japan's economy booming. Rapid industrial growth meant that the Japanese people were richer than ever before. The cities of Hiroshima and Nagasaki shared in the new prosperity. They were rebuilt and soon had larger populations than in 1945.

However, the sufferings of the survivors of the bombings (known as

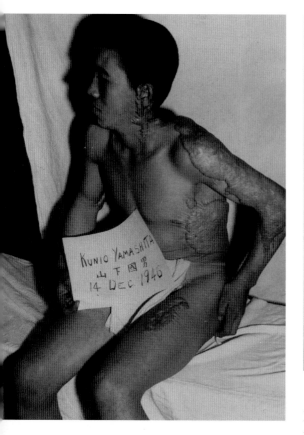

Seventeen-year-old Kunio Yamashita exhibits the raised keloid scars that disfigured so many victims of the Hiroshima and Nagasaki bombings.

VOICES FROM HISTORY

Physical and mental scars

Many survivors of Hiroshima bore thick "keloid" scars on their bodies. One woman described the fate of her daughter, suffering from radiation sickness, and her disfigured son:

"The sickness was so dreadful, but we could only look on helplessly. My daughter Nanako was so eager to live for the sake of her newborn baby, but she couldn't be saved. . . . After Nanako died, I still had my 26-year-old son Hiromi; and he had keloid scars on his head and hands. Therefore, he couldn't get married, and he tried to commit suicide several times."

Quoted in Kanzaburo Oe, *Hiroshima Notes* (Grove Press, 1996)

The Franck Report (see page 21) had predicted that the world would feel a "wave of horror and repulsion" when atom bombs were first used, but this did not happen. Perhaps people's reactions to human suffering had been dulled by the savagery of World War II. On the whole, citizens in the Allied countries responded with relief that the war had ended. They were also awed by what Truman called "the greatest achievement of organized science in history." However, a new sense of insecurity did make itself felt: people realized that what had happened to Hiroshima and Nagasaki could one day happen to London and New York.

The Soviet Union knew it had to act fast. Stalin immediately ordered his scientists and weapons experts "to provide us with atomic weapons in the

hibakusha) did not share the same improved fortune. The bombs' deadly legacy meant that the hibakusha were more likely to die from several forms of cancer, especially leukemia. And many of those mentally scarred by the event ended up commiting suicide. Fortunately, fears that radiation damage might be passed down to future generations were not true. Although radiation did harm babies in the womb at the time of the bombing, children born to survivors in later years showed no signs of abnormality.

shortest possible time." They achieved that goal in four years, assisted in no small way by information passed on by spies in Britain and the United States. The first Soviet atom bomb test was carried out in September 1949.

Relations between East and West grew increasingly tense—the Soviet Union and its former wartime allies now faced one another across the "Iron Curtain" in a hostile confrontation that became known as the Cold War—"cold" because it stopped short of direct armed conflict between the major powers. In 1949, the North Atlantic Treaty Organization (NATO) was formed. This was a military alliance between the United States, Britain, and other West European countries designed to resist Soviet expansion. In 1955, the Soviet Union formed its own alliance, the Warsaw Pact, directed against NATO.

MORE POWERFUL WEAPONS

One consequence of the Cold War was that the Americans and Soviets raced one another to create bigger nuclear bombs and more effective ways of getting them to their targets. In 1952, the United States tested the first hydrogen bomb, a device using nuclear fusion rather than fission. The explosion was about 500 times more powerful than the one that had destroyed Hiroshima. Its destructive yield was equivalent to over 11 million tons of TNT. The Soviets soon responded in kind. They produced their own hydrogen bomb, and by the early 1960s were able to explode a device 1,000

President Truman puts pen to paper in front of members of the U.S. Congress in 1949. He was signing the North Atlantic Treaty which founded the NATO alliance. The treaty stated that alliance members would come to the defense of any other member threatened with attack.

WHY DID HIROSHIMA HAPPEN?

The Cuban Missile Crisis

In 1959, Fidel Castro took power in the Caribbean island of Cuba. A communist, Castro soon allied Cuba with the Soviet Union. In October 1962, U.S. spy planes revealed that the Soviets were installing nuclear missiles in Cuba, threatening the United States. U.S. President John F. Kennedy ordered a naval blockade to stop Soviet ships carrying missiles from reaching the island. For thirteen days, the two major nuclear powers teetered on the edge of war. On October 28, however, the Soviets agreed to dismantle their Cuban missile bases. The United States and the Soviet Union have never since come as close to nuclear war.

This huge mushroom cloud is evidence of an explosion 500 times more powerful than the Hiroshima bomb. It marks the first hydrogen bomb test carried out on November 1, 1952, by the United States at Eniwetok Atoll in the Pacific. The small island of Elugelab, where the explosion was detonated, was vaporized.

times more powerful than the Hiroshima bomb. Britain, France, and China also developed nuclear weapons.

The advent of rocket technology also introduced a new element to the equation. By the late 1950s, missiles had been developed that could deliver nuclear warheads—in effect the "hydrogen bombs"—to targets thousands of miles away. No city was safe any longer. Both sides sought safety in overwhelming strength, arguing that the best way to deter a devastating nuclear strike was to threaten the enemy with even worse retaliation in reply. Twenty-four hours a day, seven days a week, missiles and bomber aircraft stood ready to deliver an instant and crushing response the instant an enemy attack was detected. The United States called this hair-raising policy for keeping the peace Mutually Assured Destruction—with the appropriate acronym MAD.

In 1962, the world did come to the brink of a full-scale nuclear war. It was sparked by the Cuban Missile Crisis of 1962 (see page 42). After this, both sides made efforts to reduce the level of risk. The Americans and Soviets put a stop to nuclear tests that had been releasing dangerous radiation into the atmosphere. And years of negotiation between 1969 and 1979 led to agreements to set a limit on the number of nuclear weapons permitted to each side. However, the size of nuclear arsenals continued to grow. By the 1980s, there were around 50,000 nuclear warheads in the world, each one many times bigger than the bomb dropped on Hiroshima.

CALLS FOR DISARMAMENT

As the threat from nuclear weapons grew, so did the public protest movement. Around the world, peace groups organized protests and demonstrations calling for nuclear disarmament. Some campaigners argued that

> VOICES FROM HISTORY
>
> ## Peace or annihilation
>
> In 1982, Jonathan Schell, a well-known campaigner against nuclear weapons, summed up the situation like this:
>
> *"There is no need to 'abolish war' among the nuclear powers; it is already gone. The choices don't include war any longer. They consist now of peace, on the one hand, and annihilation on the other."*
>
> Jonathan Schell, *The Fate of the Earth* (Jonathan Cape, 1982)

a nuclear war risked the destruction of all life on Earth. The peace movement could also point to the involvement of Hiroshima itself. A Peace Museum and a Peace Park were opened in the city in 1955 and Hiroshima Day, August 6, was commemorated there with an antinuclear protest each year.

In 1985, Mikhail Gorbachev became

The shadow of nuclear war that hung over the 1960s led to the rise of protest movements that opposed the very existence of nuclear weapons, like these supporters of the Campaign for Nuclear Disarmament (CND).

This is the Genbaku, or A-Bomb, Dome in Hiroshima. It is what remains of the former Hiroshima Industry Promotion Center, which was partially destroyed by the atom bomb that detonated almost directly above the building. The ruins have been preserved as a memorial in Hiroshima's Peace Park.

leader of the Soviet Union. His radical policies of restructuring the country led to a much better relationship with the United States. The nuclear arms race was halted; the Cold War drew to an end. The policies were controversial and unintentionally led to the breakup of the Soviet Union in 1991. Since then, ongoing negotiations between the United States and the new states that inherited Soviet nuclear weapons— chiefly Russia and Ukraine— have brought about major reductions in numbers of warheads and missiles.

In the twenty-first century the nuclear threat has changed, but it has not been eliminated. It now seems unlikely that a nuclear war between the major world powers will break out. But the greater danger now lies with the proliferation of nuclear weapons

WHY DID IT HAPPEN

An unendurable war

The scientists who drafted the Franck Report (see page 21) would probably have been surprised that nuclear weapons have not been used since 1945. They stated their belief that only "international agreement on the future control of weapons" could avoid a catastrophic nuclear war. Manhattan Project scientist Leo Szilard argued that the use of the bombs against Japanese cities would lower the threshold, making it more likely they would be used again. He wrote, "Once they were introduced as an instrument of war it would be very difficult to resist the temptation of putting them to such use [again]."

However, Manhattan Project scientific director Robert Oppenheimer reasoned that the atom bomb might act as a deterrent and prevent a Third World War from ever taking place. He said, "It did not take atomic weapons to make man want peace, a peace that would last. But the atomic bomb . . . has made the prospect of future war unendurable." It is possible to believe that the use of the two bombs on Hiroshima and Nagasaki revealed how terrible their effects were, and perhaps deterred governments from using nuclear weapons again.

Szilard and Oppenheimer quoted in Richard Rhodes, *The Making of the Atomic Bomb* (Penguin, 1986)

and the risk that they might fall into terrorists' hands. Many more countries now possess nuclear weapons, including India, Pakistan, and Israel. In the 2000s, it was a major aim of U.S. policy to prevent states such as Iran and North Korea—countries with governments the United States regarded as unreliable— from developing nuclear weapons. The possibility that a ruthless terrorist group such as al Qaeda might one day acquire a weapon illegally and develop the capacity to detonate a nuclear device was another major source of political anxiety.

The threat from the proliferation of WMD (weapons of mass destruction) is real. Yet it is some comfort to realize that, sixty-five years into the nuclear age, the only nuclear weapons ever used were the bombs dropped on Hiroshima and Nagasaki. The Americans resisted the temptation to use nuclear weapons during two large-scale wars fought in Korea (1950–1953) and Vietnam (1965–1973). Moreover, disputes in two of the world's hot spots have not boiled over catastrophically: India and Pakistan did not use them in their dispute over Kashmir, nor did Israel in its confrontation with its Arab neighbors. Yet there are no grounds for complacency. Hiroshima and Nagasaki remain a terrible lesson of what can happen when humans disregard peaceful solutions and go to war.

U.S. troops found Iraqi dictator Saddam Hussein hiding at a farmhouse south of Tikrit in December 2003. One of the main justifications given for the invasion of Iraq by American and British forces in 2003 was that Saddam Hussein was secretly pursuing a nuclear weapons program.

HIROSHIMA TIMELINE

1937
July 7: Japanese invade China

1939
August: Albert Einstein writes to President Roosevelt about the possibility of making an atom bomb

September 1: Outbreak of World War II in Europe

1941
June 22: Nazi Germany invades the Soviet Union

December 7: Japanese launch attack on Pearl Harbor

December: Manhattan Project to build an atom bomb is set up in the United States

1942
February 15: The British military base at Singapore surrenders to the Japanese

March: Japanese Americans living in the United States are moved into camps

April: The Philippines fall to the Japanese

November: Los Alamos, New Mexico, selected as the hub of the Manhattan Project

December 2: The first atomic chain reaction is achieved by scientists in Chicago

1944
September: Bomber Group 509 begins flight training to drop the atom bomb

October: Japanese pilots adopt kamikaze suicide tactics in attacks on the U.S. fleet

1945
February 14: Allied bombers cause firestorms that destroy Dresden, Germany

March 9–10: U.S. firebomb raid destroys much of Tokyo

April–June: Conquest of Okinawa costs the lives of 12,500 U.S. servicemen

April 12: President Roosevelt dies; Harry S. Truman becomes president

May 8: Germany surrenders unconditionally to the Allies

June: Emperor Hirohito gives his support to peace negotiations with the Allies

June 18: President Truman authorizes planning for an invasion of Japan, which is scheduled for November 1

July 16: The first atomic test device is exploded at Alamogordo in New Mexico

July 17: The Potsdam Conference of Allied leaders opens near Berlin

July 25: President Truman formally authorizes the use of atom bombs against Japan

July 26: The Allies call on Japan to surrender unconditionally in the Potsdam Declaration

July 28: Japanese government rejects Potsdam Declaration

August 6: An atom bomb is dropped on Hiroshima

August 8: The Soviet Union declares war on Japan

August 9: An atom bomb is dropped on Nagasaki

August 10: The Japanese indicate they are prepared to surrender if the emperor can remain on the throne

August 14: The Japanese government informs the Allies that it is surrendering

August 15: Emperor Hirohito broadcasts to the nation to announce the surrender

September 2: The Japanese leadership sign a formal surrender document

1949
September: The Soviet Union tests its first atom bomb

1952
April: Japan regains full independence

November 1: The United States tests the first hydrogen bomb

1955
A Peace Museum and Peace Park open in Hiroshima

1962
October: The Cuban Missile Crisis brings the world to the brink of nuclear war

1991
December 25: The Soviet Union falls apart